Teaching American History With
Favorite Folk Songs

by Tracey West

S C H O L A S T I C
PROFESSIONAL BOOKS

New York • Toronto • London • Auckland • Sydney
Mexico City • New Delhi • Hong Kong • Buenos Aires

For my dad, Tom Lubben, for teaching me
to love Pete Seeger and Woody Guthrie.

Credits
Journal entry by William Heyser (page 56) from *The Kittichtinny Historical Papers*
edited by Jane Dice Stone (The Kittichtinny Historical Society Society, 1978). Used by
permission of the Kittichtinny Historical Society, Mercersburg, Pennsylvania.

Cover illustration by Jill Newton
Cover design by Norma Ortiz
Interior design by Sydney Wright
Interior illustrations by Delana Bettoli
English translation of "Cielito Lindo" by Graciela Vidal
CD produced by A Gentle Wind
Performed by John Kirk—lead vocals, guitar, banjo, mandolin, fiddle, pennywhistle
Linda Schrade—lead vocals
Trish Miller—vocals, banjo, guitar
David Kiphuth—banjo, vocals
Jack Hume—dobro
Mark Murphy—bass

Product ISBN: 0-439-04387-5
Book ISBN: 0-439-30939-5

Contents

About This Book

◆ **WHY FOLK SONGS?** ◆

For some of us, there is nothing more exciting than hearing the stories of the people and events that helped shape our history. For others, it's difficult to make connections between words on a page and actual living, breathing people. For those individuals, history can seem like something distant and untouchable.

Folk songs can be used to bridge the gap between the past and the present. When we listen to them, they remind us of the very human emotions and characteristics of the people who sang them. Folk songs can be funny, clever, sad, or just plain informative.

For this reason, folk songs are a wonderful way to introduce American history topics to students or to add depth to a history unit. In this book you'll find lyrics to songs that bring to life some of the major events in key periods in United States history: the Colonial Period and the American Revolution, Westward Expansion, and the Civil War.

◆ **USING THE CD AND THE LYRICS** ◆

Each of the lyrics in the book can be reproduced on a photocopier and distributed to students. In addition, the CD that accompanies this book includes a performance of each song, enhanced by traditional period musical instruments. There are several ways to use the CD and the lyrics:

◆ **Introduce a Topic** Playing a song at the start of each new topic is one way to generate excitement among students about what they're going to learn. You might choose to play the song without an introduction and ask students to guess which history topic you're going to explore next. You might also play the song and use the information in it to discuss key facts about the topic you're going to study. When the unit is over, play the song again. What new things have students learned since they first heard the song?

◆ **Complement and Supplement** If you're like many teachers, you have tried-and-true lessons that you use each year to teach topics. Consider using the songs, and the questions and activities that accompany them, to complement these lessons. Students will be able to use the information they've learned so far to interpret the songs more easily; at the same time, they'll be learning new facts.

◆ **Create an Independent Learning Center** If you'd like to allow students to explore the songs on their own, set up a portable CD player and headphones on a small table. Create a

folder for each song. The folder might include the song lyrics, a sheet of key vocabulary and definitions, and the discussion questions. Students can choose a song they're interested in, listen to it, and answer the questions.

◆ ABOUT THE TEACHER PAGES ◆

In addition to lyrics, you'll find two pages of Teaching Activities for each song, including:

About the Song: helpful history and facts you can use when presenting the song to students

Key Vocabulary: definitions of slang terms that are no longer used, as well as other words your students may not be familiar with

Introducing the Song: specific suggestions for introducing the song to students in a fun and meaningful way

Discussion Questions: questions designed to test comprehension and to further explore issues or events raised in the song

More to Explore: one or more short, fun activities that connect with and supplement the song as well as your history curriculum

◆ CONNECTIONS TO THE STANDARDS ◆

The material in this book connects to the following social studies standards and benchmarks outlined by the Mid-continent Regional Educational Laboratory (McRel), an organization that collects and synthesizes noteworthy national and state K-12 curriculum standards.

◆ Students know patriotic songs, poems, and sayings that were written long ago, and understand their significance.

◆ Students understand how songs, symbols, and slogans demonstrate freedom of expression and the role of protest in a democracy.

◆ Students understand how democratic values came to be, and how they have been exemplified by people, events, and symbols.

◆ Students understand the accomplishments of ordinary people in historical situations and how each struggled for individual rights or for the common good.

Source: *A Compendium of Standards and Benchmarks for K-12 Education* (Mid-continent Regional Educational Laboratory, 1995).

The Colonial Period and the American Revolution

The history of what is now known as the United States began in the late fifteenth century, when European countries began to send explorers to colonize the Americas. In the 1700s Spain, France, and England laid claim to various territories in North America. Britain had 13 colonies along the Atlantic coast.

Many of the early settlers who came to the British colonies did so seeking new opportunities. Some, like the Pilgrims who settled Plymouth, Massachusetts, were seeking religious freedom from the Church of England. Others were forcibly brought here from Africa to work as slaves on southern plantations.

More than two centuries would pass before the slaves would taste freedom. In the meantime, settlers in the colonies were looking to break free from British rule. At the core of the issue was taxation without representation: Colonists were not allowed to serve in the British government or to have a say in any laws passed, yet they still had to pay taxes to Britain. War broke out in 1775. By 1783 the colonists had won the rebellion and an independent nation was formed—the United States of America.

TIME LINE

1620 The first British colony is settled by the Pilgrims in Massachusetts.

1732 The last of the 13 British colonies is founded in Georgia.

1754 The French and Indian War begins. Britain fights to take over French territories. Native Americans, fearful that the British will steal their land, side with the French against British soldiers and colonists.

1765 Colonists are angered when the British Parliament passes the Stamp Act, taxing most kinds of documents in the colonies.

1768 The British army occupies Boston.

1773 Colonists dump tea into Boston Harbor, in an event known today as the Boston Tea Party.

1775 The war begins. Colonists face off against British soliders at Lexington and Concord, Massachusetts.

1776 Colonial leaders sign the Declaration of Independence.

1777 The colonists win an important victory at the battles of Saratoga in New York.

1778 Encouraged by the victory at Saratoga, the French agree to side with the colonists. In response, Britain focuses its attention on the southern colonies, winning important victories there.

1779 Spain declares war on Britain.

1782 Tired of the expensive and unpopular war, Britain agrees to sign a peace treaty in Paris, France.

1783 The formal peace treaty is signed, making the United States of America an independent nation.

Frog Went a Courtin'

1. Oh, Froggie went a courtin' and he did ride, mm-hm.
Oh, Froggie went a courtin' and he did ride, mm-hm.
Froggie went a courtin' and he did ride,
A sword and pistol by his side, mm-hm, mm-hm, mm-hm.

2. He rode up to Miss Mousie's door, mm-hm.
He rode up to Miss Mousie's door, mm-hm.
He rode up to Miss Mousie's door
Where he had often been before, mm-hm, mm-hm, mm-hm.

3. He said, "Miss Mouse, are you within?" mm-hm.
He said, "Miss Mouse, are you within?" mm-hm.
He said, "Miss Mouse, are you within?"
"Just lift the latch and please walk in," mm-hm, mm-hm, mm-hm.

4. He put Miss Mousie on his knee, mm-hm.
He put Miss Mousie on his knee, mm-hm.
He took Miss Mousie on his knee,
And said, "Miss Mousie, will you marry me?" mm-hm, mm-hm, mm-hm.

Teaching American History With Favorite Folk Songs
Scholastic Professional Books

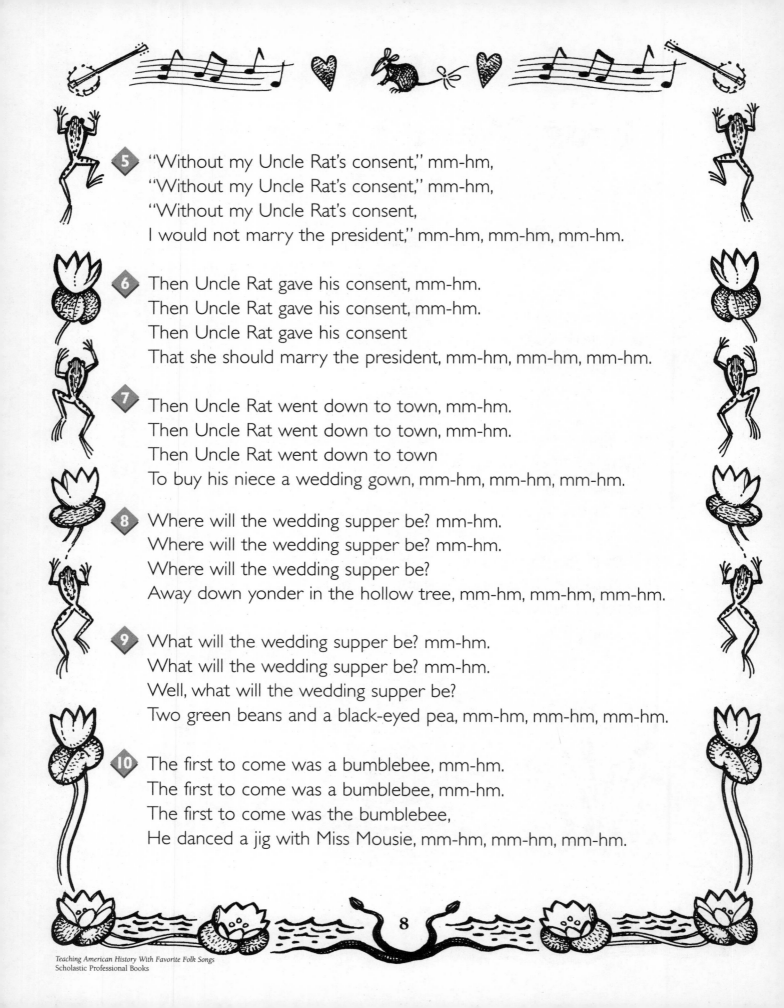

5 "Without my Uncle Rat's consent," mm-hm,
"Without my Uncle Rat's consent," mm-hm,
"Without my Uncle Rat's consent,
I would not marry the president," mm-hm, mm-hm, mm-hm.

6 Then Uncle Rat gave his consent, mm-hm.
Then Uncle Rat gave his consent, mm-hm.
Then Uncle Rat gave his consent
That she should marry the president, mm-hm, mm-hm, mm-hm.

7 Then Uncle Rat went down to town, mm-hm.
Then Uncle Rat went down to town, mm-hm.
Then Uncle Rat went down to town
To buy his niece a wedding gown, mm-hm, mm-hm, mm-hm.

8 Where will the wedding supper be? mm-hm.
Where will the wedding supper be? mm-hm.
Where will the wedding supper be?
Away down yonder in the hollow tree, mm-hm, mm-hm, mm-hm.

9 What will the wedding supper be? mm-hm.
What will the wedding supper be? mm-hm.
Well, what will the wedding supper be?
Two green beans and a black-eyed pea, mm-hm, mm-hm, mm-hm.

10 The first to come was a bumblebee, mm-hm.
The first to come was a bumblebee, mm-hm.
The first to come was the bumblebee,
He danced a jig with Miss Mousie, mm-hm, mm-hm, mm-hm.

Teaching American History With Favorite Folk Songs
Scholastic Professional Books

11 The next to come was Mister Drake, mm-hm.
The next to come was Mister Drake, mm-hm.
The next to come was Mister Drake,
He ate up all of the wedding cake, mm-hm, mm-hm, mm-hm.

12 The owl did hoot, the birds they sang, mm-hm.
The owl did hoot, the birds they sang, mm-hm.
The owl did hoot, the birds they sang,
And through the woods the music rang, mm-hm, mm-hm, mm-hm.

13 They all went sailing on the lake, mm-hm.
They all went sailing on the lake, mm-hm.
They all went sailing on the lake,
And they all got swallowed by a big black snake, mm-hm, mm-hm, mm-hm.

14 There's bread and cheese upon the shelf, mm-hm.
There's bread and cheese upon the shelf, mm-hm.
There's bread and cheese upon the shelf,
If you want anymore, just sing it yourself! mm-hm, mm-hm, mm-hm.

9

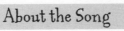
Frog Went a Courtin'

Key Vocabulary

black-eyed pea: a white seed with a black spot, similiar to a bean

courtin': dating

drake: a male duck

jig: a lively dance

yonder: over there

 About the Song

What does a song about the marriage between a frog and a mouse have to do with American history? This charming children's song is just one illustration of the customs brought to these shores by the early colonists.

The first written record of the song dates from 1580, when "A Moste Strange Wedding of the Frogge and the Mouse" was licensed to a man named Edward White in London, England. The song traveled across the ocean and over the years became popular in mountain regions, where children enjoyed creating new verses and alternate endings. Today the song is still sung to children all over the United States.

Introducing the Song

Ask students to name songs that they learned as children from friends, family, or classmates. (Name songs such as "London Bridge" to spark the discussion, if necessary.) Have they ever wondered where these songs originated? Play the CD and ask if anyone has heard the song before. Explain that this song originated in Britain, and was brought to these shores by colonists.

 Discussion Questions

- ◆ What is this song about? (*The marriage of a frog and a mouse. To extend the discussion, ask students to describe scenes in the song.*)

- ◆ Does this song remind you of any stories or books you have read? (*Answers will vary.*)

More to Explore

Sing It Yourself Invite students to accept the challenge implicit in the last lines of the song: "There's bread and cheese upon the shelf. If you want anymore, just sing it yourself!" First, discuss what they think the lines mean. Are bread and cheese important to the story the song is telling, or is it possible that the writer was just looking for something funny to rhyme with *yourself*? Then ask students to discuss the meaning of the last line. Explain that traditionally children had fun making up new verses to the song.

How do students feel about the ending, when the entire wedding party is eaten by "a big black snake"? Ask students to write a verse to replace that one, giving the frog and mouse a new fate. Brainstorm ideas as a class, and suggest that students put the new ending in rhyme.

Colonial Fun and Games Songs like "Frog Went a Courtin'" kept colonial children amused. They also played games or played with toys, and some of these are still played by children today. Most libraries are a good source for out-of-print books filled with rhymes and games played by colonial children. You and your students might find some that interest you and hold a Colonial Fun and Games Day.

To get started, make a buzz-saw toy. You'll need one 36-inch length of string and one piece of cardboard.

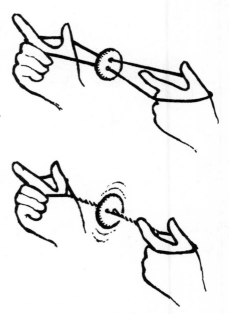

1. Cut a circle about 3 to 4 inches in diameter from the cardboard. Decorate each side, as desired. Poke two small holes in the center of the circle.

2. Thread the string through each hole, positioning the circle so that it sits in the middle of the string. Tie the ends of the string together, as shown.

3. To play, loop the ends of the string over your fingers and wind up the string with a flipping motion. Then make the circle spin by pulling the left end of the string, then the right, and so on.

Revolutionary Tea

1 There was an old lady lived over the sea,
And she was an Island Queen;
Her daughter lived off in a new countrie,
With an ocean of water between.
The old lady's pockets were full of gold,
But never contented was she,
So she called on her daughter to pay her a tax
Of threepence a pound on her tea,
Of threepence a pound on her tea.

2 "Now Mother, dear Mother," the daughter replied,
"I shan't do the thing you ax;
I'm willing to pay a fair price for the tea,
But never the three-penny tax."
"You shall," quoth the mother, and redden'd with rage,
"For you're my own daughter, you see.
And sure 'tis quite proper the daughter should pay
Her mother a tax on her tea,
Her mother a tax on her tea."

3 The tea was conveyed to the daughter's door,
All down by the ocean's side.
And the bouncing girl pour'd out every pound,
In the dark and boiling tide.
And then she called out to the Island Queen,
"Oh Mother, dear Mother," quoth she,
"Your tea may you have when 'tis steep'd enough,
But never a tax from me,
But never a tax from me."

12

Revolutionary Tea

 About the Song

On December 16, 1773, American patriots dumped 342 chests of tea into the Boston Harbor. The act was one of protest. For years, the British Parliament had placed a tax on imported tea as a symbol of its authority. To avoid paying a tax they believed to be unfair, Americans smuggled their tea from Holland. The East India Company appealed to Parliament to intervene, and the British government refunded the duty on a 500,000-pound shipment so that the East India Company could sell its tea cheaper than the smuggled tea, even though it was taxed. Boston patriots rejected this manipulation by the British government. Sixty men, dressed like Mohawk Indians, boarded a ship and dumped the tea shipment into the harbor. The event, which came to be known as the Boston Tea Party, gave new hope to the rebels in the colonies and inspired many songs.

"Revolutionary Tea" is an allegory—it uses symbols to tell the story of the tea party. The "Island Queen" is Britain, and the "daughter" is the American colonies.

 Introducing the Song

Play the song. Ask students if they can identify the historical event the song is about. Then call on students to read the song aloud, one verse at a time. Take time to go over any unusual words or spellings, and discuss them, if necessary. In the second verse, for example, *ax* is used in place of the word *ask* so that it would rhyme with *tax*.

 Discussion Questions

◆ In the song, what reason does the daughter give for dumping the tea in the tide? (*She doesn't want to pay the tax.*)

Key Vocabulary
conveyed: brought from one place to another
quoth: said
steeped: soaked in a liquid
threepence: three cents or three pennies

◆ Do you think dumping the tea was a good way for the patriots to protest the unfair tax? Why or why not? (*Answers will vary.*)

More to Explore

Boston Tea Party Filmstrip Students can bring the Boston Tea Party to life by creating a filmstrip viewer that tells the story of this event.

First, distribute the reproducible on page 15 to each student. Ask students to illustrate the events described. Explain that it's not necessary to draw detailed scenes; a representative object or face will work just fine. When they are done, students should cut out the two strips and tape panels 3 and 4 together to make one long strip. Next, students can write a script that describes the events depicted in each panel. Encourage them to write a short paragraph for each panel, adding details and relating the panels to one another. Then ask each student to bring in an empty, cube-shaped facial tissue box. Model how to make the viewers using the directions, right.

Who's Who In the American Revolution With the reproducible on page 16, students can make a flip chart that tells about some major players of the American Revolution. Make a copy of the reproducible for each student. Then lead students through these steps:

1. Cut out the chart along the outer dotted lines. Then cut along the inner dotted lines so that each question flips back.

2. Turn the paper over. Put glue or tape around the edges. Glue the paper to another piece of paper the same size. Make sure the edges meet.

3. Flip up each question and write the correct answer underneath. Use library books or the Internet to find the answers.

4. (Optional) Decorate the border with symbols or pictures from the American Revolution.

Encourage students to take home their finished flip charts and quiz friends and family members about these Revolutionary people. For an additional challenge, have students create flip charts on their own for other figures in the war, including Benjamin Franklin, Nathan Hale, Patrick Henry, Abigail Adams, Benedict Arnold, Ethan Allen, and Thomas Paine.

How to Make a Filmstrip Viewer

1. Cut off both ends of the box.

2. About an inch from each end of the box, cut a slit. The slits should run the height of the side and allow for easy passage of the filmstrip.

3. Thread panel 1 into the right-hand slit and then through the left-hand slit. To view the filmstrip, pull the strip to the left, one panel at a time.

Answers: 1. King George III 2. Paul Revere 3. Crispus Attucks 4. Betsy Ross 5. George Washington 6. Phyllis Wheatley 7. Thomas Jefferson

Name _____

Boston Tea Party Filmstrip

Draw a picture to illustrate each panel. Cut out the panels along the dotted lines. Then tape panels 3 and 4 together to make one long strip.

3 In 1773 three ships carrying tea sailed into Boston Harbor.

6 The men tossed 342 chests of tea into the water to protest the tax.

2 Sam Adams led the colonists who opposed the tax.

5 They boarded the ships at night.

1 In 1767 the British placed a tax on tea sent to the colonies.

4 Sam Adams and 60 men disguised themselves as Mohawk Indians.

15

Who's Who in the American Revolution

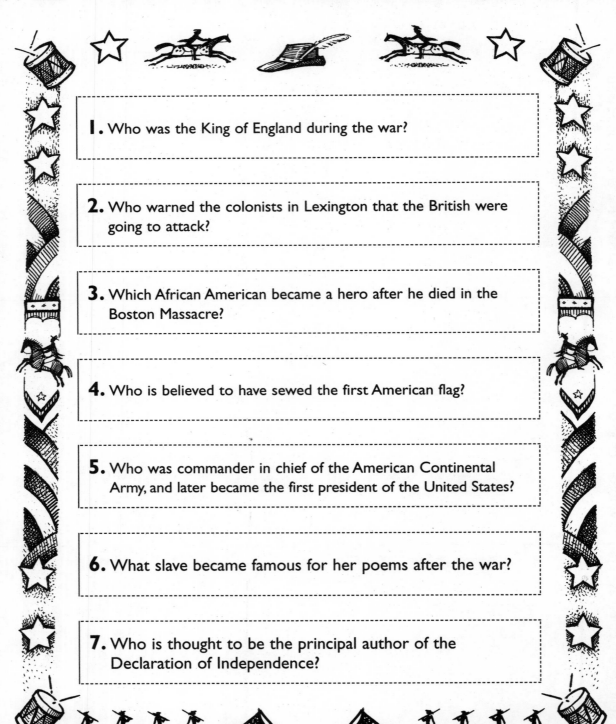

1. Who was the King of England during the war?

2. Who warned the colonists in Lexington that the British were going to attack?

3. Which African American became a hero after he died in the Boston Massacre?

4. Who is believed to have sewed the first American flag?

5. Who was commander in chief of the American Continental Army, and later became the first president of the United States?

6. What slave became famous for her poems after the war?

7. Who is thought to be the principal author of the Declaration of Independence?

Yankee Doodle

1 Yankee Doodle went to town,
Riding on a pony.
Stuck a feather in his cap,
And called it Macaroni.

Chorus:
Yankee Doodle, keep it up,
Yankee Doodle Dandy,
Mind the music and the step,
And with the girls be handy.

2 Father and I went down to camp,
Along with Captain Gooding,
And there we saw the men and boys,
As thick as hasty pudding.

3 There was Captain Washington
Upon a slapping stallion,
A-giving orders to his men,
I guess there was a million.

Chorus

4 There they had a swamping gun,
As big as a log of maple,
Upon a deuced little cart,
A load for father's cattle.

 **17**

Teaching American History With Favorite Folk Songs
Scholastic Professional Books

5 And every time they fired it off
It took a horn of powder.
It made a noise like father's gun,
Only a nation louder.

Chorus

6 And there I saw a little keg,
Its head was made of leather.
They knocked on it with little sticks,
To call the folks together.

7 There they'd fife away like fun,
And play on cornstalk fiddles;
And some had ribbons red as blood,
All bound around their middles.

Chorus

8 The troopers, too, would gallop up,
And fire right in our faces.
It scared me almost half to death,
To see them run such races.

9 But I can't tell you half I saw,
They kept up such a smother;
So I took my hat off, made a bow,
And scampered off to mother.

Chorus

10 "Yankee Doodle" is the tune
Americans delight in;
'Twill do to whistle, sing, or play,
And just the thing for fightin'.

Chorus

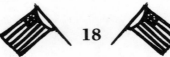

18

Yankee Doodle

 About the Song

Chances are you've probably hummed or whistled this catchy tune at some time in your life. Most people know at least the first verse, but are not so clear on what the song is about.

The song is said to have been written in 1755, during the French and Indian War. A British army doctor named Richard Shuckburg is credited with the lyrics to the first verse, which are meant to make fun of American soldiers. *Yankee* was a derisive word for someone from New England, and *doodle* was a fool. The British continued to sing the song at the start of the American Revolution, until the patriots turned the tables on them by changing the lyrics and making it a sort of anthem. Some say that the American troops made British soldiers dance to the tune; another tale says that it was played when the British army surrendered to George Washington in Yorktown in 1781.

 Introducing the Song

Ask students if they have heard the song "Yankee Doodle." What do they think it's about? Write their answers on the chalkboard. Play the song, and ask students to tell what the song describes. Explain that the song is about a boy watching American soldiers train for battle.

Go over key vocabulary with students, and discuss the song verse by verse. Explain that the song was first sung by the British, as a way of making fun of American troops. Then American soldiers turned the song into one of pride.

 Discussion Questions

◆ What are some of the things the boy sees at the camp? (*Answers may include: George Washington on a horse; "millions" of soldiers; a big, loud gun; musicians playing drums and flute to get the troops going.*)

Key Vocabulary

dandy: a man who pays too much attention to his clothing or appearance

deuced: a slang word; a modern equivalent might be *cool*

doodle: a fool

fife: a small flute; to play a small flute

hasty pudding: cornmeal mush

macaroni: a dandy; decorations on uniforms

swamping gun: a large cannon

troopers: soldiers

Yankee: a native or inhabitant of New England; originally a derisive term

◆ What kinds of things in the song might the soldiers have been proud of? (*Answers may include: their ability to ride horses and fire guns well; the fact that they possessed powerful weapons and had a strong commander.*)

More to Explore

Song Pictures Each verse of the song describes a colorful and sometimes exciting scene. However, the vocabulary and rhyme might make it difficult for some students to decipher meaning. A fun way to help students overcome this is to have them turn the verses into pictures. Write each verse on a separate sheet of paper, and divide the class into ten groups. Have each group illustrate the scene in one of the verses. Allow them to use books with pictures of the American Revolution as reference. Create an illustrated Yankee Doodle mural by displaying the pictures in order on one or more walls in your classroom and posting each verse under the appropriate picture.

"And There Was Captain Washington" The "Captain Washington" in the song is none other than George Washington, before he rose to the rank of general and was elected the first president of the United States.

Students can use the reproducibles on pages 21 and 22 to make a George Washington Fact Cube. Make a copy of both pages for each student. Have students follow the instructions on page 21 to make their cubes. Encourage students to research the facts in your class-room, your school library, or on the Internet. One good web site is <u>Mount Vernon</u> at **http://www.mountvernon.org.**

When the cubes are finished, you can stack them in a Fact Pyramid. You might also hang a string across the classroom, attach a string to each cube, and tie the cubes onto the main string in order to create a large mobile.

George Washington Fact Cube

1. Cut out the patterns on pages 21 and 22 along the outer dotted lines.

2. Fill out each panel according to the instructions below.

   Panel 1: Write your name on the line.

   Panel 5: Draw or paste a picture of George Washington.

   Panels 2, 3, 4, and 6: In each of these panels, write a fact you've found about George Washington. Illustrate each fact, if you wish.

3. Glue Tab A behind Panel 5.

4. Fold along the solid lines to form a cube.

5. Glue each tab behind the panel it meets.

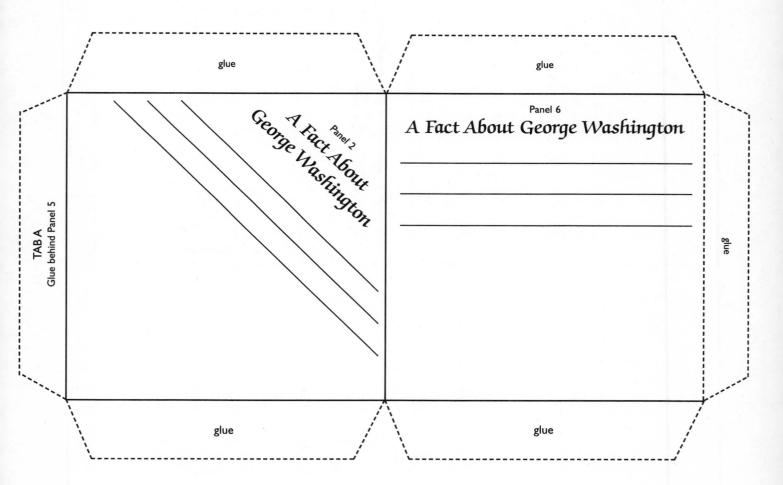

21

George Washington
Fact Cube

Panel 1

George Washington Fact Cube

Name _____

glue

Panel 4

A Fact About George Washington

glue

Panel 5

Picture of George Washington

Glue TAB A behind Panel 5

Panel 3

A Fact About George Washington

_____

_____

_____

Westward Expansion

The United States of America did not end with the 13 colonies. In 1803 President Thomas Jefferson and Secretary of State James Madison orchestrated the Louisiana Purchase. They paid French emperor Napoleon 15 million dollars for the Louisiana Territory. The land was "owned" by France and purchased by the United States, in spite of the fact that Native Americans had lived there for centuries and felt that the land belonged to them.

Around this time more and more settlers began traveling west. In doing so, they often forced Native Americans off their land. First, canals were built to make transportation easier and quicker. By the middle of the nineteenth century, the railroads were built, allowing settlers to travel even farther west. By 1850 Americans had settlements all along the Pacific Coast. Those settlements grew with the completion of the Transcontinental Railroad in 1869.

The songs in this section tell stories about the workers who made westward expansion possible.

TIME LINE

1803 The United States buys the Louisiana Territory from France in the Louisiana Purchase.

1805 Lewis and Clark, explorers sent to find an all-water route to the Pacific Ocean, reach their goal.

1825 The Erie Canal is completed.

1830 Congress passes the Indian Removal Act, allowing the government to remove Native Americans from their ancestral lands. The moves take place over a decade, and many Native Americans lose their lives.

1846 The United States declares war on Mexico in a dispute over territories in the southwest. When the war ends in 1848, the size of the United States is greatly increased.

1848 Gold is discovered in Sacramento, California, sparking the gold rush, which reached its height in 1849.

1862 Congress passes the Homestead Act, allowing settlers to keep any land they have farmed for five years.

1869 The Transcontinental Railroad is completed, allowing people to travel by train from the East Coast to Sacramento.

The Erie Canal

1 I've got a mule, her name is Sal.
Fifteen miles on the Erie Canal.
She's a good old worker and a good old pal.
Fifteen miles on the Erie Canal.
We've hauled some barges in our day,
Filled with lumber, coal, and hay.
And we know every inch of the way,
From Albany to Buffalo.

Chorus:
Low bridge, everybody down!
Low bridge, for we're comin' to a town!
And you'll always know your neighbor,
You'll always know your pal,
If you've ever navigated on the Erie Canal!

2 We better get on our way, ol' gal.
Fifteen miles on the Erie Canal.
'Cause you bet your life I'd never part with Sal,
Fifteen miles on the Erie Canal.
Git up there, mule, here comes a lock,
We'll make Rome 'bout six o'clock.
One more trip and back we'll go,
Right back home to Buffalo.

Chorus

24

The Erie Canal

 About the Song

In the early history of the United States, the transportion of goods and people from one place to another was usually a long and difficult process. The Erie Canal was one of the first efforts to make this process easier. Built between 1817 and 1825, the canal stretched from Albany on the Hudson River to Buffalo on Lake Erie. The canal made it possible to transport goods more cheaply and encouraged people to settle in new or underdeveloped areas.

Travel on the canal was slow. Mules walked on a towpath on the right side of the canal, pulling heavy freight barges that floated on the canal; horses pulled passenger boats. The original canal had 83 locks, or sections, containing gates that were opened to allow the boat to move to a higher or lower section of water.

"The Erie Canal" and other songs were sung by mule drivers in order to stave off boredom and to avoid falling asleep on the job. The cry "Low bridge!" was raised when the barge reached a town that had a walkway over the canal. If workers didn't remember to duck, they'd bump their heads!

By 1850 railroads proved to be a more efficient means of transportation and the use of the canals diminished. Nonetheless, this song has survived.

 Key Vocabulary

barge: a large, flat-bottomed boat that is usually towed

canal: a waterway created by people

lock: a section of a canal with watertight gates at each end used in raising or lowering a boat

mule: the offspring of a male donkey and a mare (or female horse)

navigated: traveled by water

Rome: in this song, a city in New York

 Introducing the Song

Ask students to imagine that there are no planes, trains, or cars. How would they move something heavy, such as a load of bricks, from one end of your state to the other? Discuss their ideas. Ask: "Would these ways be quick or effective? Who can think of a faster way?"

Explain that years ago, when America was starting to expand, people came up with an ingenious way to transport items over long distances:

They built canals. You might want to create a K-W-L chart about canals. Label the columns What We Know About Canals, What We Want to Know, and What We've Learned.

Discuss key vocabulary before playing and distributing the song. Once students have listened to the song, return to the chart. What have students learned? Was any of this information surprising to them?

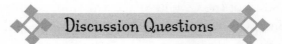

Discussion Questions

◆ According to the song, what kinds of goods were transported on barges? (*lumber, coal, and hay*)

◆ Do you think barges could be used to transport goods today? Why or why not? (*Answers will vary.*)

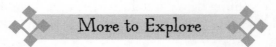

More to Explore

A Song to Pass the Time This song was written by mule drivers to help pass the time during the long, dull journey. Invite students to write a song to help pass the time during another slow or boring activity, such as waiting on line or washing the dishes. They can set their songs to the tune of "The Erie Canal."

Travel the Erie Canal! Ask students to imagine that they own a barge that takes passengers to destinations up and down the Erie Canal. How would they entice people to take the trip? Give each student a copy of the reproducible on page 27. Have students follow the instructions to create a colorful travel brochure. They can find information about the canal in libraries, encyclopedias, or on the Internet. One useful web site is The New York State Canal System at **http://www.canals.state.ny.us/**.

Travel the Erie Canal!

Create a brochure to convince people to take a barge up the Erie Canal.

1. Cut the brochure along the dotted line and then fold along the center line with the blank side facing out.

2. On the cover, draw a picture of the barge or of a beautiful sight someone might see on the trip. Give the brochure a title.

3. Inside the brochure, answer the questions. Then color the map. Color the lakes blue and trace the Erie Canal in red.

4. On the back cover, write a few lines summarizing why you think passengers should travel on your barge.

Going out West? Here's a great reason to take a barge:

_____
_____
_____
_____
_____

Along the way, you'll see these beautiful cities!

_____
_____
_____
_____
_____

CANADA

Lake Ontario

Lake Oneida

ERIE CANAL

NEW YORK

Tonawanda

Buffalo

Lake Erie

Finger Lakes

Albany

Hudson River

PENNSYLVANIA

Teaching American History With Favorite Folk Songs
Scholastic Professional Books

John Henry

1 When John Henry was a little baby
Sitting on his papa's knee,
Well, he picked up a hammer and a little piece of steel, said,
"Hammer's gonna be the death of me, Lord, Lord,
Hammer's gonna be the death of me."

2 Well, the Captain said to John Henry,
"Gonna bring that steam drill round.
Gonna bring that steam drill out on the job.
Gonna whip that steel on down, Lord, Lord.
Gonna whip that steel on down."

3 Well, John Henry said to the Captain,
"Lord, a man ain't nothing but a man,
But before I'd let your steam drill beat me down,
I'd die with a hammer in my hand, Lord, Lord.
I'd die with a hammer in my hand."

4 Now the Captain said to John Henry,
"I believe that mountain's caving in."
John Henry said right back to the Captain,
"Ain't nothing but a hammer sucking wind, Lord, Lord.
Ain't nothing but a hammer sucking wind."

Teaching American History With Favorite Folk Songs
Scholastic Professional Books

5 Now the Captain said to John Henry,
"What is that storm I hear?"
John Henry said, "Captain, that ain't no storm.
That's just my hammer in the air; Lord, Lord.
That's just my hammer in the air."

6 Now the man who invented the steam drill,
He thought he was mighty fine.
But John Henry drove fifteen feet,
The steam drill only made nine, Lord, Lord.
The steam drill only made nine.

7 John Henry hammered in the mountains;
His hammer was striking fire.
But he worked so hard, it broke his poor heart,
And he laid down his hammer and he died, Lord, Lord.
He laid down his hammer and he died.

8 They took John Henry to the graveyard,
And they buried him in the sand.
And ev'ry engine comes a-roaring by
Whistles, "There lies a steel-driving man, Lord, Lord.
There lies a steel-driving man."

9 John Henry had a little baby;
You could hold him in the palm of your hand;
And the last words I heard that poor boy say,
"My daddy was a steel-driving man, Lord, Lord.
My daddy was a steel-driving man.
My daddy was a steel-driving man, Lord, Lord.
John Henry was a steel-driving man."

29

John Henry

engine: a locomotive; motorized car that runs on rails and pulls railroad cars behind it

steam drill: a machine, powered by steam, that drives steel spikes into railroad ties quickly and efficiently

steel-driving man: a railroad worker whose job was to drive steel spikes into railroad ties

 About the Song

The history of the railroad in the United States began in 1830, when Peter Cooper designed a locomotive powered by steam. Between 1850 and 1870, thousands of miles of railroad tracks were built across the country.

Railroad workers were recruited from many walks of life; African Americans, Irish and Chinese immigrants, and Civil War veterans all worked together to build the railroads. The life of a railroad worker was filled with danger and hardship; nonetheless, when machines began to replace human labor, many workers feared for their jobs.

The story of John Henry arose from this man-versus-machine conflict. Many believe that the story is based in truth: John Henry was an African American steel driver. Sometime around 1870 he set up a race against a steam drill to prove that a man could do the job better than a machine. He died shortly after the contest (some say from a fever; others say he burst a blood vessel). John Henry's contest quickly became a legend that grew bigger and bigger with each retelling. The legend has remained alive thanks to this unforgettable folk song, which was first collected by folklore scholars in Kentucky.

 Introducing the Song

Before playing and distributing the song, explain that students are about to hear a song that may have started as a true story, but that has become a tall tale—it's larger than life. Listen to the song together, and discuss which elements of the song might be based in fact and which might have been exaggerated.

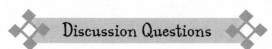
◆ Why was it important for John Henry to beat the steam drill? (*He wanted to prove that a man could do the work as well as a machine.*)

◆ What happens in verse 4? (*The captain praises the steam drill, but John Henry scoffs at the praise: "Ain't nothing but a hammer sucking wind."*)

◆ In verse 5, what does the song tell us about how hard John Henry was working? (*The captain thinks he hears a storm, or thunder, and John Henry responds that it's the noise his hammer is making.*)

◆ Who won the contest? (*John Henry; he drove the steel deeper into the ground than the steam drill did.*)

◆ What happened to John Henry when the contest was over? (*He died from working so hard.*)

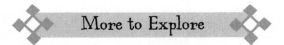

More to Explore

Map of the Western Railroads In 1869 the Union Pacific and Central Pacific Railroad companies finished their race to lay track from the Pacific Ocean to the Missouri River. The two lines met in Promontory Point, Utah, and for the first time it became possible to travel from the East Coast to the West Coast by rail. Until then, eastern rail lines had gone no farther than the Missouri River, and cross-country travel had been difficult and dangerous.

Students can explore this historic event using the map on page 32. Answers: 1. c 2. c 3. four 4. Sierra Nevada 5. Omaha, Nebraska 6. California, Nevada, and Utah Territory

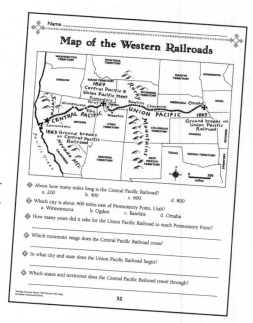

Map of the Western Railroads

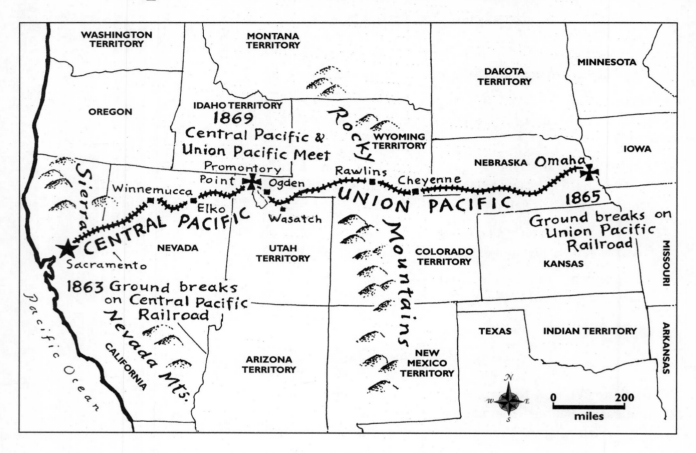

1 About how many miles long is the Central Pacific Railroad?
   a. 200   b. 400   c. 600   d. 800

2 Which city is about 400 miles east of Promontory Point, Utah?
   a. Winnemucca   b. Ogden   c. Rawlins   d. Omaha

3 How many years did it take for the Union Pacific Railroad to reach Promontory Point?

_____

4 Which mountain range does the Central Pacific Railroad cross?

_____

5 In what city and state does the Union Pacific Railroad begin?

_____

6 Which states and territories does the Central Pacific Railroad travel through?

_____

Oh, Susanna

Lyrics by Stephen Foster

1 I come from Alabama
With my banjo on my knee.
I'm going to Louisiana,
My Susanna for to see.

Chorus:
Oh, Susanna!
Oh, don't you cry for me,
For I come from Alabama with my banjo on my knee.

2 It rained all night the day I left,
The weather was so dry.
The sun so hot, I froze to death,
Susanna, don't you cry.

Chorus

3 I had a dream the other night,
When everything was still.
I thought I saw Susanna
A-coming down the hill.

Chorus

4 A red, red rose was in her hand,
A tear was in her eye.
I said, "I come from Dixie land,
Susanna, don't you cry."

Chorus

Teaching American History With Favorite Folk Songs
Scholastic Professional Books

Oh, Susanna

Key Vocabulary

banjo: a musical instrument, similar to a guitar, with a round body, a long neck, and four or more strings

Dixie land: the southern states of the United States

About the Song

In 1848, a millworker named James Marshall found gold in a stream in Sacramento, California. By 1849, thousands of treasure seekers flocked to California, lured by the promise of easy wealth. A few of the prospectors did indeed get rich, but most people left behind their homes and families only to find backbreaking work, disappointment, and danger. The "forty-niners," as they were called, risked getting robbed, murdered, or catching a disease in the often unsanitary and lawless camps.

One year before Marshall's discovery, the song "Oh, Susanna" was introduced by popular entertainer Stephen Foster. The sentimental song, with its nonsense lyrics, became popular with the forty-niners and was called the "theme song" of the gold rush.

Introducing the Song

Ask students if they have ever had to leave home for a period of time. Did they get homesick? What kinds of things did they bring with them to remind them of home?

Tell students that the song they are about to hear was a favorite of the forty-niners, men who left their homes to look for gold in California.

Discussion Questions

◆ Why do you think the forty-niners might have liked the song so much? (*Answers may include: It might have reminded them of loved ones they left back home; some of the forty-niners probably traveled to California from Dixie land; the silly lyrics might have cheered them up; the catchy tune is easy to sing along with and dance to.*)

More to Explore

A Golden Opportunity Some people who traveled to California to seek their fortune in 1849 did become wealthy—but not because they found gold. Instead, they sold much-needed goods to the miners at inflated prices. Because "boom towns" were springing up in areas that had been sparsely settled, there were not enough merchants to serve the needs of the new settlers.

Therefore, these savvy businesspeople sold goods such as food, paper, prefabricated houses, clothing, and cooking utensils. They also provided laundry services and entertainment. One man even made a living drawing portraits of the miners.

Discuss a few of these examples with students, and then ask them to think of a product or service they could provide to settlers in a mining town during the gold rush. Have students create an advertisement for their product or service. Instruct them to use language and images that will entice the miners to spend their gold dust.

Making Laws The chaos surrounding the gold rush sent California into a tailspin. What would your students do if a similar situation occurred where you live? Divide the class into groups of four or five. Ask them to imagine that gold has been discovered on an area of unclaimed land outside your city. They must assume the role of state lawmakers and create laws concerning your local gold rush. Use these questions to prompt students' discussions:

Who should be allowed to look for gold? Whoever gets there first? Only people who live in your state? Or should the land be left undisturbed so wildlife will not be harmed?

Do miners need permission to dig for gold? Should they pay a fee to the state for that permission?

Who gets to keep the profits from the gold? The people who find it? Should the state get a piece of the profits?

You've heard reports that some miners are selling "fool's gold," a metal that looks like gold but is not valuable. How would you stop or punish those people?

Ask students to draft their laws on a sheet of paper. Then have a representative from each group read the laws. As a class, discuss what each group has determined. Is the class in agreement on most issues? What issues do you disagree on? If you had to draft one set of laws as a class, how would you keep everyone satisfied?

Get Along, Little Dogies

1 As I was out walking one morning for pleasure,
I saw a cowpuncher come riding along.
Hat was thrown back and his spurs were all jingling,
And as he approached he was singing this song.

Chorus:
Whoopee ti yi yo, get along, little dogies!
It's your misfortune and none of my own.
Whoopie ti yi yo, get along, little dogies,
For you know Wyoming will be your new home.

2 It's early in spring that we round up the dogies,
We mark them and brand them and bob off their tails.
We round up our horses, load up the chuckwagon,
And then throw the dogies out onto the trail.

3 It's whoopin' and yelling and drivin' the dogies.
And oh how I wish you would only go on!
It's whoopin' and punching, go on, little dogies,
You know that Wyoming will be your new home.

Chorus

4 Some boys, they go up on the trail just for pleasure,
But that's where they get it most awfully wrong.
You haven't a notion the trouble they give us,
It takes all our time to keep moving along.

5 Your mother was raised way down in Texas,
Where the jimsonweed and the sandburs grow.
We'll fill you up on prickly pear and cholla,
Then throw you on the trail to Idaho.

Chorus

36

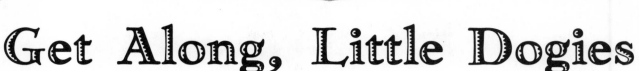
Get Along, Little Dogies

 About the Song

In the mid–nineteenth century, three million cattle roamed northern Mexico and Texas. The newly finished railroads—and some good old American ingenuity—helped to put these cattle on the dinner plates of people all over the country. Entrepreneurs who settled in the west knew they could make money selling the cattle back east, so they created a market by launching a campaign promoting beef as a delicious food. Now all they had to do was get the cattle from Texas to rail yards in Kansas, where they would be taken to northern and eastern states. That's where the cowboy came in.

These workers herded the cattle and drove them across the open ranges to Kansas. It wasn't easy work—the days were long and the trail could be dangerous. The threat of rustlers stealing the cattle or, of a stampede, were very real.

Cowboys sang many songs to pass the time. "Get Along, Little Dogies" describes the process of transporting the cattle, right down to the jingling spurs of the cowboy.

 Introducing the Song

Tell students that they are about to hear a song sung by cowboys on a cattle drive. Discuss what students know about cattle drives. Ask: "What happened on a cattle drive? Why were the cattle being moved? How did cowboys get the cattle to their destination?" Play the song and discuss the details given. Review key vocabulary. To follow up, distribute the lyrics and ask students to write a paragraph summarizing what happens on a cattle drive, based on the information in the song.

Key Vocabulary

bob: to cut shorter

brand: a mark, burned into the hide of an animal, that shows to whom the animal belongs

cholla: a spiny cactus

chuckwagon: a wagon used to carry a stove, food, and cooking equipment

cowpuncher: cowboy

dogie: a motherless calf in a herd

jimsonweed: a poisonous plant that produces prickly fruit

prickly pear: a kind of cactus that produces a pear-shaped, edible fruit

sandburs: weeds that produce a prickly fruit

spur: a spike or spiked wheel on the heel of a rider's boot, used to make a horse follow commands

whoopin': shouting

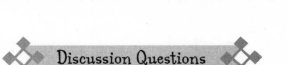

◆ Does being a cowhand sound like easy or difficult work? (*Answers will vary.*)

◆ Do you think you would have taken the job of cowhand? Why or why not? (*Answers will vary.*)

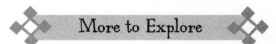 More to Explore

More Than Just a Hat It's hard to picture a cowboy or cowgirl without the trademark hat. A cowboy hat was more than just a style statement—it served many important functions. A cowboy hat shielded the cowhand's eyes and neck from the hot sun while keeping the head cool; it was a barricade against rain and snow; it protected a cowhand's head from low-hanging branches and thorns. Cowhands also used their hats to carry water, to fan fires, to discipline wild or excited horses, and as a place to rest their heads at night.

Your students can have fun discovering these uses for themselves. Divide the class into groups, and give each group a cowboy hat. (Inexpensive hats can be purchased at party supply stores or from Oriental Trading at 1-800-875-8480; **www.oriental.com**; or perhaps students can bring them from home.) Ask students to imagine that they are cowhands who have just set up camp on the prairie. Set the scene:

You rode your horse for hours in the hot sun. You rode through thorns and brambles. A sudden thunderstorm soaked your skin and scared the horses. Now it's dusk, and you're setting up camp. A clear stream bubbles nearby. You've just built a roaring campfire. You're tired, hungry, and dirty . . .

Now ask students to examine the hat. What kinds of things might a cowhand have used the hat for? Ask students to study the hat while thinking about the environment cowhands worked in and the challenges they faced. Set a timer for ten minutes. At the end of ten minutes, ask each group to demonstrate the uses they came up with. Keep a running list on the chalkboard. Add some of your own ideas, if necessary.

Cielito Lindo

(Spanish)

1 De la Sierra Morena,
Cielito lindo vienen bajando.
Un par de ojitos negros,
Cielito lindo, de contrabando.

Chorus:
Ay, ay, ay, ay!
Canta y no llores.
Porque cantando se alegran,
Cielito lindo, los corazones.

2 Pájaro que abandona,
Cielito lindo, su primer nido,
Si lo encuentra ocupado,
Cielito lindo, bien merecido.

Chorus

Teaching American History With Favorite Folk Songs
Scholastic Professional Books

Cielito Lindo

(English)

1 Down the Sierra Morena,
My pretty sweetheart, they are descending.
One pair of little black eyes,
My pretty sweetheart, they're sneaking through.

Chorus:
Ay, ay, ay, ay!
Sing and don't cry.
Because, my pretty sweetheart,
Singing gladdens the heart.

2 When a bird abandons,
My pretty sweetheart, his first nest,
If he then finds it taken,
My pretty sweetheart, he well deserves it.

Chorus

Teaching American History With Favorite Folk Songs
Scholastic Professional Books

Cielito Lindo

 ## About the Song

For years, the faces of cowboys in movies and on television were white. This image is changing to match what we now know about the real cowboy population. It's estimated that one-fifth of all cowboys were African American, and the very first cowboys were indigenous Mexicans and Native Americans.

While we often think of cowboys as free spirits roaming the plains, their history was rooted in servitude. When Spanish settlers formed missions in what is now Mexico, California, and Texas, they forced the native peoples there to work on the missions and nearby ranches. The horsemen were called *vaqueros*, from the Spanish word meaning "cow"—*vaca*.

Later vaqueros were a mix of Native and Spanish ancestry, and wealthier vaqueros wore elaborate costumes and gear on formal occasions. The word *buckaroo* referred to a cowboy who wore fancy clothes.

This traditional Spanish song, with its emotional and romantic lyrics, was a favorite of vaqueros, and the chorus is still familiar today.

 ## Introducing the Song

Ask students to describe what they think a cowboy looks like. Do they know that the first cowboys were Mexican Indians? Explain that the cowboy song they're about to hear was sung by these cowboys, or *vaqueros*, in Spanish.

Have students listen to the song once without looking at the translation. Ask: "How does this song make you feel? What do you think it's about?" If there are Spanish-speaking students in the class, ask them to explain the lyrics. If not, pass out the lyric sheet. How well do the lyrics match the music? Were students' impressions close?

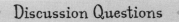

Discussion Questions

◆ The chorus of the song tells the listener to "Sing and don't cry." What does this tell you about what the life of a cowboy might have been like? (*Answers may vary, but may include:* lonely, difficult, *and so on.*)

◆ Do you agree with the statement that "singing gladdens the heart"? (*Answers will vary.*)

More to Explore

A Cowboy Tale Nat Love was an African American cowboy whose real-life adventures are said to have inspired exciting "dime novels" in the 1880s. Short stories and books about cowboys have excited readers since cowboys roamed the plains.

Cowboy legends can inspire students to write their own exciting short stories. Have them get started by reading about cowboys in books or on the Internet. (See Resources on page 62.) Then get them going with these Wild Western story starters:

"Stampede!" Charlie yelled. Then five hundred frantic cows charged the camp.

The sheriff pinned a gold star on the cowhand's chest. "Looks like you're the new sheriff now," he said.

The lookout's loud cry woke the cowhand from his sleep. "Rustlers!" he yelled. "Rustlers are stealing the cattle!"

After a long day on the trail, the cowhand slipped into a warm bedroll. Something brushed against the cowhand's bare leg. The cowhand froze. It could be only one thing— a rattlesnake!

Have students choose one of these story starters (add your own, if you like) and finish the story. When they're done, have students sit in a circle and read their stories aloud, campfire style.

The Civil War

In the nineteenth century, the United States was growing and expanding. Yet there were big differences between states in the North and the South. The South was made up of large plantations where most of the work was done by slaves. In the North people worked in factories and on small farms, and slavery was no longer practiced.

As states and territories applied for admission to the Union, the argument raged about whether slave states should be allowed to join. Abolitionists argued that new states added to the Union should not be slave states, because they felt that slavery was morally wrong and against the Declaration of Independence, which declared that "all men are created equal."

Compromises were drawn—the Missouri Compromise, the Compromise of 1820, and the Compromise of 1850—but the issue was never settled. When antislavery candidate Abraham Lincoln was elected in 1860, the southern states began to secede. Lincoln believed the Union should be kept intact at all costs. The Civil War began shortly thereafter.

TIME LINE

1833 Abolitionists form the National Antislavery Society.

1849 Harriet Tubman escapes slavery and finds freedom in the North. She becomes a leading conductor on the Underground Railroad.

1860 Abraham Lincoln is elected president, and South Carolina secedes shortly thereafter.

1861 The Confederates fire on Fort Sumter, and the Civil War begins.

1863 Lincoln issues the Emancipation Proclamation, freeing slaves in the South.

1864 Although the Confederates make headway in July, Union General William T. Sherman occupies Atlanta, Georgia, and then Savannah, Georgia, delivering a devastating blow to the South.

1865 As the Confederate army begins to fall, John Wilkes Booth assassinates President Lincoln. Less than a month later, the last Confederate army unit surrenders. The war is over.

Follow the Drinking Gourd

1. When the sun comes back and the first quail calls,
   Follow the drinking gourd.
   For the Ole Man's awaiting for to carry you to freedom.
   Follow the drinking gourd.

   Chorus:
   Follow the drinking gourd,
   Follow the drinking gourd,
   For the Ole Man is awaiting to carry you to freedom.
   Follow the drinking gourd.

2. Oh, the riverbank makes a very true road.
   Dead trees will mark the way.
   The left foot, pegfoot, traveling on.
   Follow the drinking gourd.

   Chorus

3. Now the river ends in between two hills,
   Follow the drinking gourd.
   There's another river on the other side.
   Follow the drinking gourd.

   Chorus

4. When the great big river meets the little river,
   Follow the drinking gourd.
   For the Ole Man is awaiting for to carry you to freedom.
   Follow the drinking gourd.

   Chorus

Teaching American History With Favorite Folk Songs
Scholastic Professional Books

Follow the Drinking Gourd

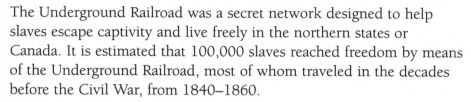

About the Song

Key Vocabulary

drinking gourd: a fruit with a hard rind; a hollowed-out gourd was used as a drinking cup

quail: a small game bird

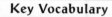

The Underground Railroad was a secret network designed to help slaves escape captivity and live freely in the northern states or Canada. It is estimated that 100,000 slaves reached freedom by means of the Underground Railroad, most of whom traveled in the decades before the Civil War, from 1840–1860.

Slaves traveling on the Underground Railroad first needed to cross the Ohio River or the eastern shore of Maryland. From there they would be escorted to northern states or to Canada. "Agents" aided escaped slaves along the way, but often slaves traveled alone. The route was dangerous, with the threat of capture always a step behind. Agents came up with secret signs and codes to help escaped slaves find the way to safe houses on the route.

"Follow the Drinking Gourd" is one example of how information was transmitted. The song provides disguised directions for reaching the North. The drinking gourd is really the Big Dipper, the constellation of stars, indicating that nighttime was the safest time to travel. The safest season was spring, when "the sun comes back and the first quail calls." The "Ole Man" was a white sailor named Peg Leg Joe, who left marks on dead trees to show the way.

Introducing the Song

Use this song to introduce or complement a lesson on the Underground Railroad. Explain that it was crucial to keep escape routes safe, so agents on the Underground Railroad came up with secret codes to pass along information. "Follow the Drinking Gourd" is one of those codes.

Pass out the lyrics. Before playing the song, challenge students to try to find the coded directions and advice as they listen to the song. Give them the first clue: that the drinking gourd refers to the Big Dipper constellation.

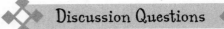

Discussion Questions

◆ When does the song say are the safest times to travel? (*At night, when the Big Dipper is out, and during the season "when the sun comes back"—spring.*)

◆ How many rivers must be followed to get to freedom? (*Three: the Tombigbee, Tennessee, and Ohio rivers.*)

◆ How do you think dead trees might have shown travelers the way? (*Answers will vary. Explain that signs were carved on the dead trees.*)

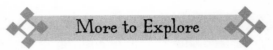

More to Explore

Heroes of the Antislavery Movement In the 1800s many brave people risked and even lost their lives in the fight against slavery. They stood up for what they believed was right and never gave up. Some of these people include Underground Railroad "conductors" such as Harriet Tubman; writers and speakers such as Frederick Douglass, Harriet Beecher Stowe, and Sojourner Truth; and ministers such as Lucretia Coffin Mott.

Students can use books and the Internet to research one of these heroes or another of their choice. (A great web site is **http://www.biography.com**. Also see Resources on page 62.) Give each student a copy of the reproducible on page 47. Students can draw or paste a picture of their chosen subject in the square and write a paragraph summarizing his or her accomplishments on the lines provided. Post the finished pages on a bulletin board or wall to create a Wall of Heroes.

Writing in Code The lyrics to "Follow the Drinking Gourd" are cleverly coded directions to a route on the Underground Railroad. Challenge students to create a set of coded directions of their own. Suggest that they try a simple route, such as from school to home or from home to a friend's house. If possible, have students exchange directions with others who are familiar with the area to see if they can guess where the route takes them.

Hero of the Antislavery Movement

Hero's Name:

_____

Hero's Accomplishments:

_____
_____
_____
_____
_____
_____
_____
_____
_____
_____
_____
_____
_____
_____
_____

Teaching American History With Favorite Folk Songs
Scholastic Professional Books

Dixie Land

by Daniel D. Emmett

1 Oh, I wish I was in the land of cotton,
Old times there are not forgotten.
Look away, look away, look away, Dixie land.
Oh, I wish I was in Dixie, Hooray! Hooray!
In Dixie land I'll take my stand
To live and die in Dixie.
Away, away, away down south in Dixie.
Away, away, away down south in Dixie.

2 In Dixie land where I was born in,
Early on one frosty mornin'.
Look away, look away, look away, Dixie land.
Oh, I wish I was in Dixie, Hooray! Hooray!
In Dixie land I'll take my stand
To live and die in Dixie.
Away, away, away down south in Dixie.
Away, away, away down south in Dixie.

48

Dixie Land

  About the Song

On December 20, 1860, South Carolina became the first state to secede from the Union. The Civil War began four months later, when the Confederate army attacked Fort Sumter. By June 1861, a total of 11 states seceded to form the Confederacy.

In 1859, as dissension between the North and South grew, a musician named Daniel D. Emmett penned the song "Dixie Land." The song grew in popularity, and when it was performed at an event in New Orleans, it became an anthem of the people. It was sung at the inauguration of Confederate president Jefferson Davis in 1861. "Dixie Land" inspired the Confederate Army as well, and was sung by soldiers on the battlefield.

Key Vocabulary

Dixie: a term for the southern states, especially the Confederate states. The term comes from the word "dix," which means "ten" in French. The ten-dollar bills used by the French-speaking people of Louisiana were printed with the word "dix" on the back.

 Introducing the Song

In the song, Dixie Land is called "the land of cotton." Ask students if they know why the southern states may have been called that. Explain that the fact that the southern states grew crops, including cotton, sugar, and rice, was one of the reasons the North and South argued. The southern states argued that slaves were needed to work on cotton plantations, while the northern states wanted to abolish slavery.

Inform students that the song became one of the songs most beloved by Confederate soldiers.

 Discussion Questions

◆ Why do you think the Confederate army might have been inspired by this song? (*Answers will vary.*)

◆ The song has a catchy tune. But can you find any lyrics that support that idea that the Southerners felt seriously about their ideas? (*"In Dixie land I'll take my stand to live and die in Dixie."*)

A Nation Divided Between December 20, 1860 and June 8, 1861, 11 states seceded from the Union to form the Confederacy. Students can use the reproducible map on page 51 to see how the differences between the Confederacy and the Union physically divided our nation. After you pass out the map, ask students: *Does this map look different from a modern map of the United States? What are the differences?* (Alaska and Hawaii are missing; there are territories instead of states in the Midwest and parts of the Northwest.) Explain that this is what the United States looked like in the Civil War era. Then ask students to follow the instructions on the reproducible.

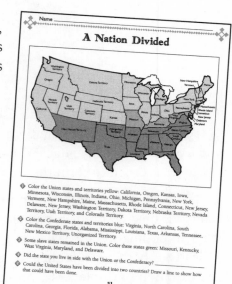

Comparing North and South As you progress through your studies of the Civil War, your students will discover many facts in the songs contained in this book, as well as in other curriculum materials. The graphic organizer on page 52 can help students sort out the facts that differentiate the northern states and the Union from the southern states and the Confederacy. Let students fill in the information as they go along, or assign the page as an independent research project.

Answers: **Union:** President Abraham Lincoln; believed slavery should be illegal; General Ulysses S. Grant; small farms and factories; believed the Union should be kept together.
Confederacy: Jefferson Davis; slavery should be legal; General Robert E. Lee; farms and plantations; believed states should have the right to secede.

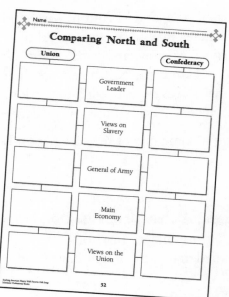

A Nation Divided

◆ Color the Union states and territories yellow: California, Oregon, Kansas, Iowa, Minnesota, Wisconsin, Illinois, Indiana, Ohio, Michigan, Pennsylvania, New York, Vermont, New Hampshire, Maine, Massachusetts, Rhode Island, Connecticut, New Jersey, Delaware, New Jersey, Washington Territory, Dakota Territory, Nebraska Territory, Nevada Territory, Utah Territory, and Colorado Territory.

◆ Color the Confederate states and territories blue: Virginia, North Carolina, South Carolina, Georgia, Florida, Alabama, Mississippi, Louisiana, Texas, Arkansas, Tennessee, New Mexico Territory, Unorganized Territory.

◆ Some slave states remained in the Union. Color these states green: Missouri, Kentucky, West Virginia, Maryland, and Delaware.

◆ Did the state you live in side with the Union or the Confederacy? _____

◆ Could the United States have been divided into two countries? Draw a line to show how that could have been done.

51

Teaching American History With Favorite Folk Songs
Scholastic Professional Books

Comparing North and South

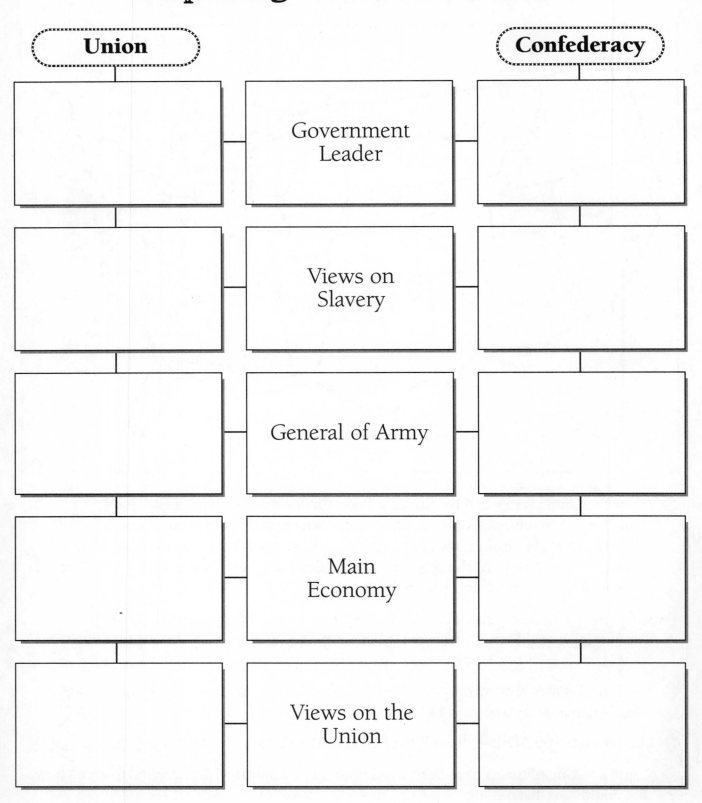

Union

Confederacy

Government Leader

Views on Slavery

General of Army

Main Economy

Views on the Union

When Johnny Comes Marching Home

Lyrics and Music by Patrick S. Gilmore

1 When Johnny comes marching home again, Hurrah! Hurrah!
We'll give him a hearty welcome then, Hurrah! Hurrah!
The men will cheer, the boys will shout,
The ladies they will all turn out,
And we'll all feel glad when Johnny comes marching home.

2 Get ready for the Jubilee, Hurrah! Hurrah!
We'll give the hero three times three, Hurrah! Hurrah!
The laurel wreath is ready now,
To place upon his loyal brow,
And we'll all feel glad when Johnny comes marching home.

3 In eighteen hundred and sixty-one, Hurrah! Hurrah!
That was when the war begun, Hurrah! Hurrah!
In eighteen hundred and sixty-two,
Both sides were falling to,
And we'll all feel glad when Johnny comes marching home.

4 In eighteen hundred and sixty-three, Hurrah! Hurrah!
Abe Lincoln set the slaves all free, Hurrah! Hurrah!
In eighteen hundred and sixty-three,
Old Abe he set the slaves all free,
And we'll all feel glad when Johnny comes marching home.

5 In eighteen hundred and sixty-four, Hurrah! Hurrah!
Abe called for five hundred thousand more, Hurrah! Hurrah!
In eighteen hundred and sixty-five,
They talked rebellion and strife;
And we'll all feel glad when Johnny comes marching home.

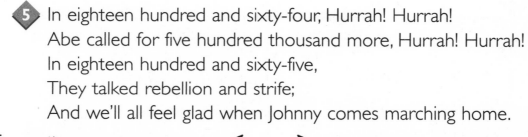

Teaching American History With Favorite Folk Songs
Scholastic Professional Books

When Johnny Comes Marching Home

◆ Key Vocabulary ◆

laurel wreath: a wreath made of laurel; an herb, worn by soldiers victorious in battle

strife: a bitter fight between enemies

About the Song

Although the first battle of the Civil War was fought in 1861, the war had its beginnings in 1860, when Abraham Lincoln was elected president. Lincoln wanted to stop the southern states from seceding, and he wanted to stop the spread of slavery to new states. Lincoln became the hero of the Union army, and an inspiration to Union soldiers.

"When Johnny Comes Marching Home" celebrates Lincoln, the heroism of soldiers, and milestones in each year of the Civil War. The song was written by Patrick Gilmore, a Union army bandmaster. It continued to be a favorite anthem of soldiers long after the Civil War ended.

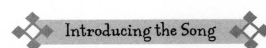

Introducing the Song

If possible, play "Dixie Land" (see page 48) before playing this song. Once students have explored the point of view of the southern states, tell them they're going to hear a song that was a popular anthem of the northern, or Union, states. Explain that the "Johnny" in the title represents all soldiers who fight bravely in battle. Ask students to listen closely and to use their lyric sheets to find facts about the war.

Discussion Questions

◆ In the song, what does the line "Abe called for five hundred thousand more" mean? (*Lincoln was calling for more troops to fight the Confederate army.*)

◆ Why do you think this song was popular with soldiers in other wars? (*Answers will vary.*)

Civil War Time Line Go through the song verse by verse with students, pausing at each year. Ask: "What milestone does the song describe in each year? Is the information always specific?"

Have students continue what the song started and create a Civil War time line. Give each student an unlined index card or sheet of paper (depending on how much wall space you have). Divide the class into five groups, and assign each group a year from 1861–1865.

Tell students to write the year they were assigned in bold writing at the top of the card. Students can position the cards vertically or horizontally when they write. Then have students use books or the Internet to research events that took place during that year. (A great web site for this activity is **http://www.civilwar.com**. Also see Resources on page 62.) Tell students to write a sentence describing the event on the card and include a specific date, if possible. Make sure each card contains a different fact.

When the cards are done, work with students to put the events in chronological order. To make a vertical time line, punch two holes in the top and bottom of the cards and use yarn to connect them. (For a horizontal time line, punch holes in the sides of the cards.)

One Day in the War Songs such as "When Johnny Comes Marching Home" can give us a unique glimpse into the minds and hearts of the people who lived during Civil War times. Historians are also fortunate to have many letters and diaries from that time. The journal entry of William Heyser on reproducible page 56 is just one example.

Before passing out the reproducible, discuss the ways in which modern historians learn about the past. Ask: "What sources might historians look at to find out what happened in the past?" (*Answers may include: songs, photographs, letters, journals, legal records, newspaper accounts, and in the 20th and 21st centuries, film and video.*) Pass out a copy of the reproducible to each student and explain that the journal entry was written by a man named William Heyser, a banker who lived in Mercersburg, Pennsylvania. On October 10, 1862 his town was taken over by Confederate soldiers, or *Rebels*. From this short paragraph, they can learn a lot about what it was like to live during the war. Review vocabulary such as *cavalry, artillery, provisions, requisitioned,* and *secreted.*

Answers: 1. Heyser seems worried about what might happen, but not terribly frightened. He talks about the rain before he talks about the Rebel invasion and he slept soundly that night. 2. Horses and provisions can help the army in battle. 3. to keep the townspeople from sending messages for help 4. He sent his horses away with "Proctor," presumably a friend or servant. 5. No. Heyser says they "conducted themselves orderly." 6. Answers will vary.

One Day in the War

This journal entry was written by William Heyser, a banker who lived in Mercersburg, Pennsylvania. Read the entry and then answer the questions below.

October 10, 1862

Rain today. A great saving for farmers who were facing a great [draught]. Business is flourishing in town. The Rebels are in Mercersburg, and on the way to Chambersburg from St. Thomas. This evening they entered our town, demanding its surrender. Some 1,500-2,000 calvary, with some artillery. They immediately took possession of the bank and the telegraph office. Also requisitioned provisions, clothing, etc. as to their needs. It has all happened so quickly, we all felt safe knowing the Union Army was in Williamsport, Maryland. The Confederate troops all look well fed and clothed, and so far, conducted themselves orderly. They will be busy stripping our stores and gathering up horses. I have sent my three off with Proctor, I hope they got away safely. I did not go to bed until after one o'clock, watching what may happen after all retire. So far, all quiet. Secreted some of my most valuable papers and went to bed, slept soundly until morning.

1 How does William Heyser feel about the Rebel invasion?

_____

2 Why do you think the Rebels are emptying stores and stealing horses?

_____

_____

3 Why do you think the soldiers took over the telegraph office?

_____

_____

4 How did William Heyser keep his horses from being stolen?

_____

_____

5 From this journal entry, do you get the impression that the Confederate soldiers harmed anyone in Mercersburg? _____

6 On the back of this paper, write William Heyser's journal entry for October 11. Write what you think happened in Mercersburg the next day.

Just Before the Battle, Mother

Lyrics by G. F. Root

1 Just before the battle, Mother,
I am thinking most of you;
While upon the field we're watching,
With the enemy in view.
Comrades brave around me lying,
Filled with thoughts of home and God;
For well they know that on the morrow
Some will sleep beneath the sod.

Chorus:
Farewell, Mother, you may never
Press me to your heart again;
But oh, you'll not forget me, Mother,
If I'm numbered with the slain.

2 Hark! I hear the bugle calling,
'Tis the signal for the fight;
Now may God protect us, Mother,
As He ever does the right.
Hear the "Battle Cry of Freedom,"
How it swells upon the air!
Oh yes, we'll rally 'round the standard,
Or we'll perish nobly there.

Chorus

Teaching American History With Favorite Folk Songs
Scholastic Professional Books

Just Before the Battle, Mother

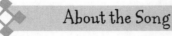 About the Song

The Civil War saw the highest death toll of any United States war. More than 600,000 Americans died in the conflict.

Unlike a typical rousing battle song, "Just Before the Battle, Mother" reflects the fear of every soldier going into battle: that he might die, never to see home and family again. This song was sung by officers in both the Confederate and Union armies, a sad reminder that despite our differences, humans share many of the same hopes and fears.

Introducing the Song

Ask students to imagine that they are soldiers in the Civil War. In the morning, they will face enemy troops. What kinds of emotions might they be feeling? Explain that this song expresses the thoughts and feelings of a soldier who imagines talking to his mother on the eve of battle. Review key vocabulary before playing the song. .

Discussion Questions

- Why do you think the soldier is "thinking most" of his mother before the battle? (*Answers will vary.*)

- What does it mean when the soldier says the troops will "rally 'round the standard, or we'll perish nobly there." (*They'll do their best to fight for what they believe in, even if it means they'll die trying.*)

- How does this song make you feel? (*Answers will vary.*)

More to Explore

A Letter to Lincoln For thousands of years, people have fought wars to settle conflicts. This song drives home the sad realities of war and provides an opportunity for students to think about the topic. Ask: "Is war the best way to solve problems?" Tell students to think about what they know about the Civil War. Then have them imagine that it is 1862. Ask students to write a letter to Abraham Lincoln explaining their view of the war. Ask: "Should the war continue? Why? If not, what solutions do you have for bringing the war to an end?" Suggest that students support their argument in the letter.

Four Score and Seven Years Ago . . . One of the most famous speeches in American history was delivered at a memorial for fallen Civil War soldiers. Abraham Lincoln gave the address on November 16, 1863 in Gettysburg, Pennslvania, the site of a three-day battle in which thousands of soldiers lost their lives. Reading the Gettysburg Address with students is a wonderful opportunity to explore primary source material.

Give each student a copy of the reproducible on page 60. Begin by reading the address aloud, reviewing challenging vocabulary: *endure, consecrate, conceived, hallow, resolve.* Then give students a chance to read the speech silently to themselves and answer the question. When students are done, discuss their answers and their impressions of the speech. Ask: "How does Lincoln feel about the deaths of the soldiers? What does he think needs to be done to honor their memory?"

This activity also makes a great take-home activity. Ask students to read and discuss the address with a family member.

The Gettysburg Address

Four score and seven years ago our fathers brought forth on this continent a new nation, conceived in liberty and dedicated to the proposition that all men are created equal. Now we are engaged in a great civil war, testing whether that nation or any nation so conceived and so dedicated can long endure. We are met on a great battlefield of that war. We have come to dedicate a portion of that field as a final resting-place for those who here gave their lives that that nation might live. It is altogether fitting and proper that we should do this. But in a larger sense, we cannot dedicate, we cannot consecrate, we cannot hallow this ground. The brave men, living and dead who struggled here have consecrated it far above our poor power to add or detract. The world will little note nor long remember what we say here, but it can never forget what they did here. It is for us the living rather to be dedicated to the great task remaining before us—that from these honored dead we take increased devotion to that cause for which they gave the last full measure of devotion—that we here highly resolve that these dead shall not have died in vain, that this nation under God shall have a new birth of freedom, and that government of the people, by the people, for the people shall not perish from the earth.

What is the main idea that Abraham Lincoln was trying to express with this speech? Write your answer below.

_____

_____

_____

_____

_____

_____

Wrapping Up

Here are some suggestions for putting the songs and lessons in this book together at the end of your American history unit:

◆ **Make a U.S. History Songbook** Copy the lyrics for each song and use a stapler or a hole punch and yarn to make a class songbook, or have students make individual songbooks. Students can create a cover and illustrations for each of the songs.

◆ **Hold a U.S. History Musical Revue** Divide the class into groups, and assign one song to each group. Ask each group to practice singing its song with the CD (or with the help of a pianist), and then present all the songs to parents or other classes. To take it further, students can act out or pantomime the song. They can also create period props and costumes to accompany their performance.

◆ **Graph Your Favorite Song** Which song did your class like best? Find out by creating a simple graph. On a large piece of posterboard, draw horizontal lines so that you have a bar for each song you've shared with the class. In each bar, write the name of one song. Then have students write their name on a self-sticking note and stick their name next to the song they liked best. When all votes have been cast, have students study the graph. Ask: "Which song was the most popular? the least? Was it a close race for first place? Did you have to count the names, or could you tell just by looking at the length of the names in each bar?"

◆ **Take It Further** Challenge students to find more songs—on CDs, audiotapes, or in books—that tell about different periods, events, or lifestyles in American history. Open it up to include events in the twentieth and twenty-first centuries. Suggest that they talk to parents or grandparents about songs they remember or know. Then have students present their findings to the class.

Resources

THE COLONIAL PERIOD AND THE AMERICAN REVOLUTION

Daughter of Liberty: A True Story of the American Revolution by Robert Quackenbush (Hyperion Books for Children, 1998)

Fireworks, Picnics, and Flags by James Cross Giblin (Houghton Mifflin, 1983)

Hasty Pudding, Johnnycakes, and Other Good Stuff: Cooking in Colonial America by Loretta Frances Ichord (Millbrook Press, 1999)

If You Lived at the Time of the American Revolution by Kay Moore (Scholastic, 1998)

If You Lived in Colonial Times by Ann McGovern (Scholastic, 1992)

WESTWARD EXPANSION

The Amazing Impossible Erie Canal by Cheryl Harness (Simon & Schuster, 1999)

Gold Fever! Tales From the California Gold Rush by Rosalyn Schanzer (National Geographic Society, 1999)

Gold Rush!: The Young Prospector's Guide to Striking It Rich by James Klein (Tricycle Press, 1998)

The Transcontinental Railroad (Cornerstones of Freedom) by Peter Anderson (Children's Press, 1996)

True Heart by Marissa Moss (Silver Whistle, 1999)

THE CIVIL WAR

Aunt Harriet's Underground Railroad in the Sky by Faith Ringgold (Crown Publishing Group, 1995)

Civil War Days: Discover the Past with Exciting Projects, Games, Activities, and Recipes by David C. King (John Wiley & Sons, 1999)

The Last Safe House: A Story of the Underground Railroad by Barbara Greenwood (General Distribution Services, 1998)

A Picture of Freedom: The Diary of Clotee, a Slave Girl (Dear America series) by Patricia C. McKissack (Scholastic, 1997)

Shades of Gray by Carolyn Reeder (Simon & Schuster, 1999)

Strange but True Civil War Stories by Nancy L. Clayton (Lowell House, 1999)

Sweet Clara and the Freedom Quilt by Deborah Hopkinson (Alfred A. Knopf, 1995)

◆ WEB SITES ◆

The Amazing Colossal Cruise Through Time and History
http://library.thinkquest.org/2834/
Take a time machine ride and see the signing of the Declaration of Independence.

The Civil War
http://www.civilwar.com
Loads of information, including a time line, in an easy-to-navigate format.

The Civil War Home Page
http://www.civil-war.net/
Read actual letters and diaries of soldiers.
Includes a lesson plan.

Erie Canal Village
http://www.eriecanalvillage.com
Check out this web site to see photos of the canal.

The Gold Rush
http://www.pbs.org/goldrush
This PBS site has a guide for teachers as well as fun facts just for kids.

Gold Rush!
http://www.museumca.org/goldrush/
A site from the Oakland Museum of California.
Contains a teaching guide.

Liberty! The American Revolution
http://www.pbs.org/ktca/liberty
An online companion to the PBS documentary.
Check out the fun trivia game.

The New York State Canal System
http://www.canals.state.ny.us/
This site includes comprehensive maps and history.

Notes